Gaslighting Recovery Guide

How to Recognize the Signs and Stop Manipulative Behavior in an Emotionally Abusive Relationship with a Spouse, Friend, Boss, Co-Worker, or Parent

Victoria Hoffman

© **Copyright 2021 - All rights reserved.**

The content contained within this book may not be reproduced, duplicated or transmitted without direct written permission from the author or the publisher.

Under no circumstances will any blame or legal responsibility be held against the publisher, or author, for any damages, reparation, or monetary loss due to the information contained within this book, either directly or indirectly.

Legal Notice:

This book is copyright protected. It is only for personal use. You cannot amend, distribute, sell, use, quote or paraphrase any part, or the content within this book, without the consent of the author or publisher.

Disclaimer Notice:

Please note the information contained within this document is for educational and entertainment purposes only. All effort has been executed to present accurate, up to date, reliable, complete information. No warranties of any kind are declared or implied. Readers acknowledge that the author is not engaged in the rendering of legal, financial, medical or professional advice. The content within this book has been derived from various sources. Please consult a licensed professional before attempting any techniques outlined in this book.

By reading this document, the reader agrees that under no circumstances is the author responsible for any losses, direct or indirect, that are incurred as a result of the use of the information contained within this document, including, but not limited to, errors, omissions, or inaccuracies.

Table of Contents

Introduction

Chapter 1: What is Gaslighting?

  Where Does Gaslighting Happen?

  Evidence of Gaslighting

Chapter 2: The Gaslighter

  Are Gaslighters Everywhere?

  Gaslighters and Clinical Personality Disorders

Chapter 3: Acknowledgment and Self-Compassion

  Breaking Away

  Practicing Self-Compassion

Chapter 4: Building Self-Esteem

  Reclamation

Chapter 5: Establishing Boundaries

  Countering Attacks and Reinforcing Boundaries

Chapter 6: Self-Care

  You've Got a Friend in You

Chapter 7: Establishing Healthy Relationships

Conclusion

References

Introduction

"It's you. It's definitely you."

"Can't you do anything right for once?"

"What good are you, really?"

"Why do you have to overreact all the time?"

How often have you heard sentences like these? How many times do you remember being called emotionally fragile? When was the last time you remember doing something, but were made to believe that you made a complete mess of it? Worse still, were you told that you were incapable of doing it?

"I'm not the bad guy here."

"So suddenly it's my fault that you screwed up?"

"I never intended it like that, so stop harping on it."

"I was only making a joke."

Such statements sometimes come to us not from complete strangers or people who are conflicted with our success, but from our loved ones, our friends, our family, our spouses... essentially the people we care about a great deal and thus really don't want to believe the worst of. We remain under a delusion that they could never wish us wrong, and certainly not make us question our own sanity, our emotional stability, or even our abilities to do the things we know we can do well.

And if you've thought until now that this is normal behaviour, be warned that it is not. In fact, this is gaslighting. And this isn't normal. You've actually been a victim.

"You're so insecure."

"You're being way too paranoid for your own good."

"Your emotional security is non-existent."

"Someone's being overly dramatic today."

Of all the painful and abusive behaviours one can be subjected to, gaslighting is one of the most abhorrent. It is a deliberate form of mental or even physical abuse used to exploit a person's insecurities and manipulate them into believing that they are in the wrong. And as we noted above, this can come from the people who are the closest to you since they have intimate knowledge of your personality and insecurities to actually exploit them.

"You're just exaggerating this."

"Stop blowing things out of proportion."

"Why do you need to overthink everything?"

"Maybe you're not remembering things correctly."

There are no limitations to where gaslighting can occur., Aside from your personal life, people in your workplace such as your colleagues, your managers, your career counselors even can be responsible for bullying you into having a negative opinion of yourself. In professional situations, gaslighting actually becomes impossible to avoid as you cannot always do much against a manager or supervisor, or even your co-worker. Ignoring them does not particularly help, as they are people you are in constant communication or collaboration with, which makes it even easier for them to continue to torment you with their manipulative ways.

"You never used to be like this, you know."

"You've changed a lot ever since we got together."

"You're not really making any sense to me anymore."

"Maybe you should get yourself some psychiatric help."

So how exactly are you supposed to overcome this? What steps can you take in order to minimize the damage that has been done or is being done to you? Can you reduce or even eliminate contact with them so that they don't get another chance to inflict more damage? There are so many steps and commitments one can make in order to come out of the vicious cycle that they have been subjected to—whether consciously or unconsciously—and become more confident and productive members of society. They can do all that without having to be defined by the opinions of others and the impression others create for them in society.

But first, in order to achieve this, it is important to understand that none of it is your fault. None of it comes down to who you are as a person. Who you are as a person is unique and something to be treasured and respected, and thus you should have the love and admiration of everyone in your orbit.

So take this journey to discover just what you've gone through, see how it has affected you, but most importantly, learn how to heal yourself and become more appreciative of the person you truly are.

Chapter 1: What is Gaslighting?

In 1944, a movie called Gaslight starring Ingrid Bergman and Charles Boyer showcased a phenomenon of psychological manipulation. The movie, itself an adaptation of a stage play of the same name, tells the story of a woman, played by Bergman, being made to believe that she is slowly going insane in the comfort of her own home through extensive psychological manipulation. This included manipulating her environment, the tasks she did on a daily basis, and her own opinions over things she was an expert at. And all of this was being done by her husband, played by Boyer, whose own controlling nature illustrated the lengths a man could go to in order to drive someone toward insanity.

But what sets this manipulation apart from the other kinds of psychological trauma is the fact that the woman was helplessly in love with her husband, and therefore could not stand to believe that her own husband would treat her this way. If anything, all she could believe was that he would only be looking out for her welfare and best interests, which made it easier for the man to continue his manipulation, as he would say that all he ever wanted to do was protect her. In short, nothing could be further from the truth.

Why is it called gaslighting, though? Being set in Edwardian London, the movie took great advantage of the gas light fittings inside the house, which were used to illuminate the city in the hours of the night. And with no limits to the extent of his psychological manipulation, the husband would utilize these very gas lights by flickering them low and high to create a sense of fright as well as helplessness within the woman. Thus the term gaslight has entered the common vernacular as it is known today.

Now ask yourself this: Has this ever happened to you? Certainly, you have not been subjected to flickering gas lights in your house, but what about all the rest? Being put in a position where you question your own memories, your expertise, your emotional state, and even your sanity? Gaslighting is the kind of emotional abuse that is perpetrated by loved ones or people we have in our lives in order to create self-doubts and an inherent belief that our own worth amounts to nothing. And if done for extended periods of time, gaslighting can cause irreparable psychological damage.

Where Does Gaslighting Happen?

No kind of relationship is off-limits to gaslighting. Both our personal and professional lives are susceptible to it—not just mentally, but also physically, emotionally, sexually, and even financially. Even though most overt examples of abuse including being yelled at, physically threatened or hit, gaslighting takes it all a step further. How? By making it appear as if none of this is happening. Or even if it is, it is all the victim's fault. And even if it isn't, that this is actually normal behaviour done out of supposed love by the abuser, or gaslighter in this case.

It gets even worse when threats such as withholding finances or sexual fulfillment also enter the picture, as these are indeed necessary for personal sustenance. Being rendered unable to manage your own expenses such as food, clothing, education, health and medicine, personal care and the like is one thing, but being left without fulfillment of your sexual cravings for extended periods creates a deep level of frustration and desperation that may force the victim to seek out any kind of reprieve; much like an addict who's trying to kick the habit. All of this is overwhelming enough to make the victims believe that these actions being committed by a gaslighter are supposed to be for their own good. Not only that, this behaviour is presented as essential to them as people and for their relationships. So deep are the seeds of self-doubt sown that realizing what is actually happening to the victims may take a long, long time.

Evidence of Gaslighting

Though very difficult to notice outright considering the psychological strain the victim is put under, there are tell-tale signs of gaslighting that one must always be aware of in order to recognize their debilitating effect in the long run. A common sign is the use of denial in order to confuse a victim, wherein a gaslighter categorically refuses to acknowledge they've said or done anything wrong, despite you hearing it with your own ears or witnessing it with your own eyes. No matter if there is proof of their lies, a gaslighter will manipulate the reality of the situation in their own favor and make it appear as though this accusation by the victim is a figment of their imagination with no basis in reality. Gaslighters are so confident in their abilities that even recorded conversations can be made to be taken out of context in their world.

This pattern of denial by lying about obvious abuse evolves further into more lies about the victim themself. Not only that, but gaslighters can also cause the victim to believe that these lies are a long-running pattern, making victims question their claims or why they had these doubts in the first place.

This can also be attributed to gaslighters deflecting their own shortcomings onto you, so that you are made to believe that it is all your fault. For instance, they may suggest their own infidelity is due to your own sexual inadequacies. They may even use loved ones against the victims and make them believe that maintaining a healthy support group such as friends, cousins, siblings and so on is not in the victim's best interest. It is very likely that close friends and siblings can recognize the gaslighter's behavior when the victim cannot, and it is in the gaslighter's own best interest to drive a wedge between them. They'll create feelings of envy, mistrust, ill-will, or apathy in the victim's social circle, while at the same time also create feelings of dependency, reliance, and attachment for themselves. Thus, a victim will be led to believe that their social contacts show no interest in their well being or even jeopardize their relationship with the gaslighter, and will have nowhere to turn to when the abuse gets out of hand.

More often than not, gaslighters are quite charismatic and charming. They do this by using pleasant conversations that make victims fall into a false sense of security, such as offering praise or appreciation. For all the times they will berate and belittle you, they will also provide positive reinforcement by highlighting some positive aspects of you as a person. Such praise or appreciation serves gaslighters only so that you do not immediately notice their other abuse. In fact, this appreciation creates a subtle way for them to continue manipulating you and getting their goals accomplished.

Chapter 2: The Gaslighter

Subtle, charming, confident, outgoing, charismatic, and even alluring. These are some of the traits of a gaslighter, not to mention the tools of their trade when it comes to committing emotional and even physical abuse against hapless victims who are completely enthralled by them. Because underneath their polished and appealing veneer, a gaslighter is a narcissistic, manipulative person who utilizes every single piece of their victim's life to exploit and damage them emotionally, resulting in devastating consequences.

Though it is not in itself a personality disorder, a gaslighter propagates an inherent desire to be in control of a situation and creates an aura of authoritarianism. They create an untarnishable image of themself in the minds of their victims, in which no fault can ever be found in their personality. Rather, the victims are made out to be the ones who are so full of faults and failings that it is only through the supposed benevolence of their gaslighter that they have any importance whatsoever.

Because of their controlling nature, gaslighters are ready to exploit their victims to achieve their own ends without having to make any effort on their part. They could be someone who exploits their spouse for financial stability by using their hard-earned money for their own frivolous, and often irresponsible, expenses, or even a manager or supervisor at work who psychologically manipulates hard-working employees and takes credit for all their work to enhance their own career trajectory. And worst of all, they commit all this wanton abuse by instilling a sense of gratefulness in their victims. They make them believe that these actions are being done for the victims' own good, and thus they should actually be thanking them.

As we saw earlier, gaslighters isolate their victims from an already established support base or social circle. The goal here is to debilitate the victim's ability to think for themself or make their own decisions. Controlling every aspect of their social life, from what to wear or which events to attend to what friends to meet and who to hang out with, puts the gaslighter in the driver's seat of the victim's life. They want nothing short of total control and use all their personality traits as well as abilities in manipulation to distance their victims from any possibility of getting help.

Are Gaslighters Everywhere?

Gaslighters can be found in any area of your life, particularly in marriages or engagements, and even in other non-committal emotional relationships such as casual dating, friends with benefits, etc. Spending more time together provides a gaslighter more avenues to alienate the victim from their social circles.

Any attempts by a victim to have any control over their life is dashed by the gaslighter in such relationships. In cases of infidelity, gaslighters often convince their partners that they are mistaken, despite evidence to the contrary. If a victim were to confront their tormentor, they would simply be brushed off and reminded of all that they have because of the gaslighter. The emotional dependence that has been created provides a gaslighter with far more room to leave a victim doubting themself as well as living in the fear that they will be left all alone if they continue this line of confrontation.

Other relationships, such as between parents and children, can also have one or more gaslighter in them, and surprisingly, it can work both ways. Impressionable young children can fall victim to parents who seem to be able to do no wrong for them, and therefore ignore the manipulative behaviour that would affect them mentally, emotionally, financially, and—in incredibly severe cases—sexually. Able and financially stable parents can also fall victim to their near adult or adult children who make them feel inadequate for taking care of themselves. Gaslighters in this case can use the aging parents and their naturally waning capabilities to convince them that they need round-the-clock medical attention, thereby taking them out of their comfort zones and into nursing homes. This is out of their need to take control of any financial assets, or even because they don't want to take care of their parents when they grow older and more senile.

Even in the workplace where victims don't normally have emotionally dependent relationships to speak of, gaslighting can take place at the hands of people in positions of authority. Gaslighters at work will cause victims to take their eyes off the target and lose track of their actual tasks as they begin to question themselves due to the mistakes that have been pointed out against them at work. Because they are often in positions in a managerial or supervisory capacity, gaslighters know they have the advantage of not being contradicted by their subordinates, which makes it easier for them to push their agenda onto them. For instance, a gaslighter can reprimand a victim for a job they were told to do, even when there was no such directive given. Meanwhile, the hapless victim has absolutely no clue what they are talking about, but such is the manipulation and overwhelming position of the gaslighter that the victim is forced to lower their head in failure. Often, the gaslighter reprimands the victim for not doing the job correctly, falling behind schedule on key deadlines, creating incorrect reports or statistics, missing important meetings and the like. None of these may even be true or may perhaps be exaggerated, which is exactly what the gaslighter is an expert at: Bending the truth in every conceivable way possible for their own gains.

Gaslighters and Clinical Personality Disorders

Although being a gaslighter in itself is not a common psychological order, it has been observed that most gaslighters have at least one or more kinds of clinical personality disorder, such as narcissistic personality disorder or even antisocial personality disorder, which is commonly referred to as sociopathy or psychopathy. A gaslighter with narcissistic personality disorder would already have a higher opinion of themselves and thus would feel no trouble in exerting their influence and abuse to a hapless victim. Creating an aura of awe and inflated sense of self-esteem is purposefully done in order to keep their victims in their thrall. This makes it easier for the gaslighter to gain total control and manipulate the victims' circumstances and environment to their own ends, even if the victims believe that they do this for their own good. That is actually how a gaslighter will operate.

Similarly, gaslighters will also showcase traits of sociopathy and psychopathy, as evidenced by their lack of concerns for others' well-being as well as any sense of empathy and emotional attachment with anyone else. They follow a cold and calculated regimen of methodically enhancing and progressing their own interests completely at the expense of those who have come to rely on them. Sociopaths inherently dislike the notion of being a part of a circle and therefore will not allow any such attachments for the victims they are gaslighting. Though they can be counted on to be physically violent, not everyone with an antisocial personality disorder acts with physical malice. Nevertheless, in extreme cases as those with psychopaths, physical violence can even result in fatal consequences if their antisocial and gaslighting tactics are not spotted early on.

Chapter 3: Acknowledgment and Self-Compassion

Because the debilitating nature of gaslighting leaves very little room for a victim to understand what exactly is happening to them, their thoughts, actions, feelings and emotions begin to undergo a drastic change from a state of confidence and self-assuredness to that of skepticism and self-doubt. Knowing what they were once capable of before they ever got into the orbit of a gaslighter becomes a distant memory, as they begin to believe that their past lives held very little meaning compared to the one the gaslighter is now providing to them. In reality, the gaslighter is subjecting them to a vicious form of deprogramming as it were, where a physically and mentally confident individual becomes a shell of their former selves.

In the absence of a sustaining social circle thanks to the efforts of the gaslighter to isolate them, the victims are unable to realize the changes taking place in their personalities till it is too late. However, even under dire circumstances without any outside intervention, a victim may retain some natural form of self-identity, which may ignite a spark of self-preservation.

Breaking Away

It's important to understand that gaslighting is emotional abuse. It can leave any reasonably sane person wondering about their place in the world as well as their self-worth, not to mention their ability to trust others and their intentions with them. Such is the control that gaslighters have over them that victims sometimes regard any genuine and persistent attempts from others to help them as threats to their relationship with the gaslighter. Unfortunately, ignoring such help can have devastating effects on the victims' physical and mental well-being, not to mention that the prospect of being torn away from their gaslighter is a thought that is far too unnerving for them.

In order to break free from the never-ending abusive cycle of gaslighting, a victim must first acknowledge that they are, indeed, a victim. Because of the unassuming and discrete manner with which gaslighting takes place, the victims will have to act fast in order to acknowledge that they are in an abusive relationship. There are several questions that one can ask themselves to find out if they are in fact being subjected to gaslighting. Being in a position where one has to second guess themselves or wonder whether they have an incredibly sensitive nature can lead to questioning their social and mental abilities, as well as being confused about the passage of time or their own sanity. More often than not, they will believe they are going crazy or already have, and despite having a nagging suspicion of something not being right in their lives, they will continue to believe that their happiness depends only on the benevolence of their gaslighters. Not only will this make them indecisive and hopeless, it will also lead them to make excuses and apologies for their tormentors when the gaslighting behaviour is pointed out by immediate family members, friends, and members of the social circle.

Once they begin to come out of the haze of self-doubt with an opinion that is contrary to how their lives are moving under a gaslighter's influence, the next stage is acknowledging that this behaviour is not just wrong, but is also toxic in every way. Even if you begin to notice how this behaviour is beginning to change you for the worst, this doesn't mean that the gaslighter is going to change. It not only requires a realization that this behaviour is mentally and emotionally debilitating, but also needs the victim to put their own holistic well-being first and foremost. Only then will they be able to overcome the abuse they have been subjected to.

Beginning to unshackle oneself from the chains of a gaslighter will require efforts on the part of the victim to reach out to friends and family members, thereby reestablishing the social circle they had been forced to disregard. This is vital if one is to return to the real world and regain a semblance of their old personality, their confidence, and their place in the world. Seeking out help in the form of a licensed therapist or even an anonymous support group can also help to let out what you have had to endure and bottle up through the time spent with a gaslighter. Discussing the trauma that was inflicted can no doubt be unsettling, however it is a natural and gradual process that can result in lifting a heavy weight off of one's shoulder. A professional therapist is the best person to air out all such thoughts in a safe environment, not to mention also provide you with support and an action plan to retake your life by becoming more confident and self-assured once again.

Practicing Self-Compassion

Self-compassion is the ability to care for yourself in the same way that you would care for others, such as your close friends and family members. The need for self-compassion takes root in the fact that we often find ourselves being more encouraging and compassionate towards our friends and loved ones whenever they succeed or need a shoulder to cry on. However, when it comes to us, we find ourselves brutally self-judging and self-criticizing. We nitpick our own failings and deficiencies to the extent that we no longer appreciate ourselves for all our wonderful achievements. And to a gaslighter who is looking to exploit you, a lack of self-compassion is a sure-fire first step on the road of your own undoing.

To understand what self-compassion is, it is also important to understand what it isn't. Firstly, self-compassion does not mean self-judgment. Rather, it is more of how one can be kind to oneself. Trying to motivate yourself means that you are ready to provide yourself a pep talk. Which means that this dose of self-motivation needs to be littered with kindness and appreciation. Thus, it has to be motivational as well as inspirational, the kind of thing that you would say to a friend who is down in the dumps. What it shouldn't be is something that would drive your friend towards further despair, so nothing that is demotivating, destructive, and filled with spite. Be kind to yourself just as you would be to your own grandma.

Speaking of friends and family, we have also looked at how important the role of a strong social support group is. Human beings do not just come together when they share a common happiness or joy, but also in times of grief and failure. Because the gaslighter has already alienated you from your circle of friends and family, you may be skeptical in turning to them for help, especially since your previous encounter may not have been pleasant. However, do not forget that you're only human, and it is never too late to ask for help.

And before we forget about how doubting yourself has done no favors for you to be more self-compassionate until now, how about you take a moment and see if you can actually flip the script with it. You should understand and identify the moments where you tend to think or react negatively to a situation that does not help you in any way. But instead of actually carrying out your negative thoughts or reactions, try to do the exact opposite of this. If you normally lash out and shout out your frustrations with something, how about taking a deep breath and approaching the problem with a smile? Instead of beginning to doubt yourself over a mistake that you make, you should realize that this is the only way you will be able to do it right. After all, understanding that a mistake is simply an obstacle to get from where you are to where you need to be should be enough for you to overcome your hesitation and give it another try. This is the only way one can actually achieve their goals, especially if it is going to lead to a more compassionate and forgiving self.

Above all else, it is important to remember that what you went through with a gaslighter was a painful and tortuous experience, but it is one that should make us stronger for having survived it. What we can do now to appreciate this is to shower ourselves with care and warmth, so that we feel loved where it matters the most.

Chapter 4: Building Self-Esteem

One of the most detrimental acts that a gaslighter performs on their victims is the ruthless and systematic destruction of any kind of self-esteem and self-worth they may have had before they entered such an abusive relationship. More than likely the victims' willingness to be dissected in such a manner may have played a part in it, but gaslighters do not let such concerns worry them. So, it's not just important to rebuild the sense of self-esteem you once had, but also getting used to the idea that you used to be a confident, assertive, and energetic individual. And also that you can be one again.

Regaining one's self-esteem isn't exactly a walk in the park. In fact, the sudden torrent of emotions one gets after breaking away from an abusive relationship such as one with a gaslighter can be extremely overwhelming. On the one hand, you may find yourself liberated and ready to find yourself and who you should be, but on the other hand, the methodical abuse you were subjected to leaves you with self-doubt over whether or not you can cope with this new dynamic. This can also lead towards negative thoughts, and, in the worst case scenarios you may even contemplate going back to the gaslighter and to a life that is comparatively more controlled.

Nevertheless, allowing such negativity inside will lead towards further self-deprecation and will not be helpful in any way if you're to build your self-esteem. It's important to recognize the value of our self-worth. As we progress toward increasing our level of self-esteem, we start feeling better about ourselves and start creating a resilience within us. This resilience is vital if we ever find ourselves in situations when we might be prone to common emotional attacks, including failure, rejection and stress. With better self-esteem, we can recuperate from such attacks more rapidly and be less prone to anxiety.

Of course, working on self-esteem is a tricky proposition, especially for someone who has already experienced abuse. A particular point to realize is that self-esteem can fluctuate wildly, whether it's on a daily or even hourly basis. Not only that, there are a wide variety of external factors that affect our self-esteem as well, such as the value of one's profession or their efforts. Preparing a meal at home for your family and watching them make an unusual face can make one feel quite small. Watching your manager twitch and slowly shake his head as they go over a report you prepared will definitely start tearing down the self-worth one has cultivated for themselves. It causes lasting damage to the sense of one's identity when they are made to feel inadequate at the things they do well.

Furthermore, it is great to have high self-esteem, but too much of something doesn't always result in everything becoming right. Self-esteem is no different, and increasing it to levels that you may not necessarily need can make one feel overconfident and shallow. Such is the case with gaslighters themselves, particularly those with narcissistic personality disorder, as their high self-esteem can be part of the reason that they try to control others. Because of the idea that they value themselves more than the average person, they may respond a lot more defensively and even aggressively, which can hamper their professional and psychological development.

Reclamation

Despite this, it wouldn't do well to dwell upon what you shouldn't be doing, but rather focus on how much to improve your self-esteem. Some techniques, such as positive affirmations and developing your key competencies, go a long way towards building self-esteem. Repeatedly reminding yourself of how talented and capable you are puts you in a positive frame of mind and ready to take on the challenges that come your way. These are helpful as they pull you out of the pit of despair and self-deprecation you have found yourself in, and give you a reality check of what possibilities await you in the future. It also encourages a sense of humility when we reaffirm our strengths based on what we know we are capable of.

Similarly, it isn't enough to just say what you feel you can do, but actually go ahead and perform as well. By achieving our goals and realizing exactly what we are claiming to be good at, you provide your self-esteem the much-needed boost to make you feel a lot better about yourself. Depending on the kind of things you like, you should make a conscious effort to go ahead and practically apply your new-found confidence. If you have a penchant for creating art, start painting or drawing to your heart's delight. If you feel the need to be better physically, then set goals for your physical fitness and work on achieving them one step at a time. Ultimately, don't just know what you're good at, do what you're good at. Only by using our competencies practically and regularly can we hone our craft and ourselves, thus improving a great deal from where we were before.

It is also important to eliminate the lingering bit of self-doubt we may have received from our gaslighters. Because of the subtle nature of gaslighting overall, we become wary of even the tiniest bit of appreciation no matter how genuine it may be. So in situations where you are actually performing well, you may end up taking any compliments coming your way with a grain of salt. Accepting compliments can make us uncomfortable, but it is imperative that you don't brush them off. It is much better to develop a knack for accepting compliments. Responding to them with simple thanks and a smile, or even by saying, "That is so kind of you to say…" will boost your self-esteem as well as give an idea to the other person that you understand the situation. Often, these compliments are exactly what we need for self-validation, and thus we should always be receptive and welcoming to good feedback. Once we carry on with this, our initial self-doubts over the intentions of the complimenter will begin to disappear and you'll notice significant changes within your self-esteem.

Being self-critical, on the other hand, dashes any of the efforts you make to reclaim your self-worth. This is where self-compassion comes in to remind you of the best friend you have within you who is ready to treat you with more kindness. So, keep self-criticism at bay and replace it with self-compassion and kindness so that you avoid the destructive capacity of critical thoughts.

Above all else, keep in mind that improving and rebuilding self-esteem is an arduous process that will require time and dedication. Creating healthy habits for your emotional well-being and sustaining them are key to building greater psychological and emotional resilience.

Chapter 5: Establishing Boundaries

Gaslighting is a form of abuse that takes a devastating toll on its victims. By its nature, gaslighting is meant to break down a person's defenses so subtly and yet aggressively that one can never get any room to catch their breath. Gaslighters start off with lying, which sets the tone for all that is to come. Lying about irrelevant things basically threatens the boundaries people set mentally for expecting nothing but honesty. This blatant attack on how you perceive what is real and what is not can make you question reality.

Another form of vicious attacks on the boundaries you set for yourself is being constantly labeled as something inappropriate by a gaslighter. For instance, if you are overweight, then a gaslighter will make a crude remark about your weight or eating habits. But the attack doesn't stop there, and if you start to reprimand them about saying such hurtful things, a gaslighter will simply say they were only joking. They will drop all pretense of seriousness and begin to sound jovial and expect you to start laughing with them too. And when you don't, they will come back with more remarks targeting you and claiming you're far too sensitive to take a joke.

Even if they say it was meant purely in jest, which it very likely wasn't, a gaslighter has already succeeded in crossing a personal boundary by launching a direct attack on you with a hateful statement. The intended purpose of the remark has been accomplished and the victim has felt the sting of the words used against them. These verbal daggers attack the mental boundary a person sets, as they make them feel uncomfortable, insecure, and emotionally wounded. Developing countries sometimes see women in positions of self-sufficiency and financial independence being berated for their inability to devote time to their families and households. Thus their major successes are overshadowed by another aspect of their lives, which can make them lose their self-esteem and confidence in other aspects where they are performing better.

This can also lead a gaslighter to accuse you of not meeting vague and even unrealistic expectations. Often, they will lay out an accusation without providing just cause or evidence of whether their claims hold any merit. But the manner and exaggeration with which they state it hampers your ability to reason with them and it will make you start second-guessing your actions. Their expectations are constantly changing based on your answers to them. If you provide them one justification, they will turn back and change the definition of what they meant and make it appear as if you are blowing things out of proportion.

All this does is lets your gaslighter cast doubts over how you perceive the situation. Their actions only serve to puzzle and confuse you and make you feel that you are failing at the gaslighter's expectations. These expectations usually range from devoting more time or energy at home to providing more money, and can also change without any prior notice or discussion with you. For instance, they may revise the amount of earnings you are expected to bring in every month or increase the amount of chores that you may have on your to-do list. If you object, they may simply tell you that this is perfectly normal and has been for quite a while. This revision of expectations coupled with blatant lying makes a victim question the very nature of the relationship.

And once such a disagreement occurs, a gaslighter will resort to blaming you for making them angry or upset. Taking the above example once again, the gaslighter will remark emphatically that this confusion has made them upset enough to act out or even lash out. More to the point, they will lay the blame of this squarely on your shoulders for ruining their mood and creating unnecessary conflict. They will remind you of all the lengths they go to to ensure that the relationship remains healthy, when in reality they only wish to keep the relationship beneficial for themselves. In any event, the gaslighter will not respect your boundaries if it means ensuring their needs are met. Thus, logic and common sense do not come into play so long as you remain under their firm control.

Countering Attacks and Reinforcing Boundaries

One very important thing to understand is that the gaslighter will often seek to cross personal boundaries with or without the consent or knowledge of the victim. Because the gaslighter is often someone the victims know, it is simply a matter of when and not if for them to break through their defenses using a wide variety of manipulation techniques. More than likely, the victim is in such awe of the gaslighter that they seek their constant approval, which even means that they lay themselves out like a physical, mental and emotional punching bag. Therefore, it is solely up to the victim to understand that such attacks on their very person can leave them a shell of their former selves, devoid of any self-confidence and self-esteem. And the only way to counter such abuse is to take control of themselves from the gaslighter.

The first and foremost requirement is to identify manipulative and toxic traits in order to stop them dead in their tracks. This includes behaviours, actions, and remarks that cause you emotional trauma, mental anguish, and also affect your physical health. Once you realize that these are attacks, you can resolve to strengthen your boundaries against the gaslighter, and call them out on their actions. If they attempt to manipulate you by threatening to cut off communication and leave you isolated, it is in your best interest to actually take action rather than pander to them for their forgiveness. Giving them a taste of their own medicine is all it takes to reassert control over your own life and putting them on the defense for a change.

Now you may actually be wondering whether doing this could be considered a kind of gaslighting against the gaslighter. In a way, it is. However, as long as it is done in order to establish boundaries that do not threaten you emotionally or mentally, reasserting yourself in the eyes of your abuser is a declaration of your own self-worth and will make them think twice before they act against you again. But let's not forget about how too much self-esteem can actually be a negative thing, and therefore it is important to remember that the goal is your emotional well-being rather than distressing someone else, even if they are a gaslighter.

Ultimately, however, if a gaslighter persists in exerting their influence over you in order to gain total control, it may be high time to put an end to such a relationship once and for all. Seeking guidance from a licensed therapist or a support group can provide you with a proper action plan in order to terminate things with an abuser, and therefore it may be the only way you finally reassert boundaries to your well-being and begin to live a normal, happier life.

Chapter 6: Self-Care

The question you should be asking yourself at this point is this: Isn't it about time you are a friend to yourself?

Showing kindness and compassion to yourself is not entirely different than showing the same kindness or compassion to others. Practicing self-care requires you to treat yourself the same way as you would someone else when they would go through a hard time or failure. Because when something like this happens to you, you would like for someone to provide you with the kind of care and affection that you would show to others. But believe it or not, loving yourself enough to provide the kind of comfort and support you need is the kind of self-care that should come as normal behaviour to you. The famous proverb "charity begins at home" couldn't hold more true in this situation, as who better to receive your care than yourself?

More often than not, we are too critical when it comes to ourselves In fact, our instinctive reaction happens to be critical simply because we might hold ourselves to higher standards. It only takes a friend or colleague or loved one to actually swoop in to save you from the doldrums of self-loathing. This is especially true in the case of a victim of gaslighting who has been constantly reminded of their own inadequacies time and time again. Their ability to care for themselves is severely diminished, and because of their reliance on a gaslighter for fulfilling an emotional attachment, they won't see a way out for themselves until they are saved by someone else.

To understand self-care, it doesn't hurt to realize just what caring for others means in the first place. In order to care for someone, it is vital to notice their suffering in order to be in a position to alleviate it. Empathizing with someone down on their luck, such as a homeless person on the street, can make you realize just how different both your circumstances are, and yet how a cruel twist of fate could easily put you in their shoes. Recognizing this is essential if you are to figure out just how you could be moved by the suffering of others. This is the only way you are able to respond to their pain with warmth, care, and an innate need to improve someone's circumstances.

Therefore, self-care requires that you understand the position you are in similarly to how you would understand the position someone else is in. This way, you are able to treat yourself a lot more kindly just like you would with a colleague who made a crucial mistake in a quarterly presentation. Because you could have been in their place facing the same circumstances, you will want to treat them sensibly and sensitively rather than resorting to judgement or harsh remarks. The German word 'schadenfreude,' which literally means the pleasure derived from someone else's misfortune, should not apply to a situation when you see a friend or a peer in a boat that perhaps you found yourselves in not so long ago. If anything, it should make you more empathetic to their plight and offer a shoulder to cry on. This shouldn't just be out of a sense of pity, but rather a genuine understanding of one's plight based on your own experiences and understanding.

Once you understand the process that you follow naturally for helping someone else out, it doesn't take too long to apply that to yourself. There will be setbacks, as attempting to show care to yourself after having endured emotional trauma such as gaslighting will require a lot of deprogramming. You'll have already been programmed by the gaslighter to not spare yourself when it comes to criticizing your action—or failures and imperfections as stressed by the gaslighter—and also judging your own personality through a lens of self-doubt, self-loathing, and with a complete absence of self-worth. When confronted with such setbacks and misfortunes, it is important to remember that you are not perfect, and therefore should not hold yourself to such a high standard.

Inculcating a sense of genuine happiness about who you are and what your place in the world is becomes a real expression of self-care. This happiness doesn't just exist because you have started to care for yourself and want to try and fix your shortcomings, but it also exists because you have come to terms with the person you are and what makes you unique in the world. You recognize your personal qualities, your strengths and your weaknesses, and you endeavor to radiate your uniqueness for others to notice and appreciate. They will start to take notice of how you react positively to any praise or even criticism that is hurled towards you, as you recognize just what you are capable of and continue on the path that will lead towards achieving your personal and professional goals.

Setbacks will definitely occur; in fact, they are part and parcel of the constant struggle to hold onto our places in the world. Nothing is ever handed out on a silver platter, and encountering frustrations, mistakes and hardships will no doubt make you question your own self-worth once again. It is only human to react to such situations with pessimism; however, only through approaching these setbacks with a positive outlook and an optimistic attitude can you truly open yourself to make genuine improvements or changes. Once you realize that you, and you alone, can turn things around for yourself, you will find it a lot easier to treat yourself with more care and affection.

You've Got a Friend in You

There may have been a time in your lifetime where you had an imaginary friend. It might have been a manifestation of all the lessons you learned growing up, or even a subconscious voice guiding you between right and wrong. Our busy lives and schedules, as well as our social evolution while turning into adults, may have diminished the need for having such an imaginary friend. Nevertheless, it isn't entirely impossible for that subconscious voice to reemerge and help you through some trying times. Creating a line of communication between yourself and an imaginary friend may actually help you have discussions you have always thought of having with someone but couldn't. Most likely it is because you may have been afraid of the answers. But surprisingly, talking to an imaginary friend can actually open up some incredible insights that you never knew existed in you before, or may never have stumbled upon otherwise.

If talking to an imaginary friend sounds far-fetched, not to mention a little awkward, there are more subtle ways to communicate such thoughts. Writing is a powerful method wherein you can actually let your subconscious run wild with all the thoughts you have been repressing until now. It could be something as simple as a reminder or a post-it note telling you to be more kind to yourself, or warning you against possible abusive behavior coming your way. Taking it a step further, you could write an actual letter or email to yourself expressing all that you have been holding back for whatever amount of time you choose. To spice things up some more, schedule to send yourself this email at a later time, or even post a letter to yourself if possible, and be amazed when you receive it. The sudden shock of reading what your subconscious tells you can be illuminating as well as invigorating.

Using an imaginary friend to help you become more caring toward yourself can also tone down your propensity to be self-critical. Ideally, the voice you read or hear will remind you of the harm such negative thinking has caused, which means you will be able to tell yourself exactly the kind of thoughts you need to focus on. Shifting your thoughts from pessimistic, critical, and even vitriolic, to ones that are more positive, compassionate and loving makes expressing your thoughts using your subconscious voice a wholly satisfying exercise.

Writing down your feelings lets you express a whole lot of emotional depth, whether it is the subconscious pouring out the negativity and abuse you experienced at the hands of a gaslighter, or jotting down the solutions you came up for yourself during your time in an abusive relationship that you were constantly burying deep within layers and layers of your subconscious. Maintaining a journal, and logging everything that has happened to you, may at first be a trigger for reliving all the pain, the trauma, and the emotional hurt that you have had to endure, but in a way it is also therapeutic. It will make you witness first-hand just how bad things had got and may serve as a reminder to never let yourself fall in a similar position in the future. If you ever feel confident and open enough, not to mention trusting enough, to let others read from your journal, it may even serve to help others who have gone through similar trauma. It can offer other victims of gaslighting some much-needed insight into what options they have available to them, courtesy of someone who has already managed to escape. Furthermore, the feeling of being able to help others will provide a significant boost to your own self-worth, and the satisfaction that you are making a difference.

Chapter 7: Establishing Healthy Relationships

In the previous chapter, we looked at the importance of developing a more positive relationship with yourself in order to exercise self-care and kindness that you would most assuredly need in order to overcome the emotional trauma of abuse such as gaslighting. Of course just establishing a friendly and empathetic relationship with yourself won't be the only healthy bond you'll be forming on your journey to reclaim your identity. It will also be important to find your way back into relationships you had once shunned or forced to do away with because of the negative influence of a gaslighter, and now it is high time to seek out the kind of companion who will celebrate you for who you are.

Since humans are social animals driven toward connections wherever we go, healthy and positive relationships are the key ingredient for us to lead happier and healthier lives, as well as being more satisfied with ourselves thanks to the company we keep. Finding ourselves in supportive and motivating relationships helps us to see ourselves in the eyes of others and how they perceive our positive qualities, while also caring about us enough to let us know when we may be pushing our boundaries. Instead of the more exaggerated and hurtful methods employed by a gaslighter, a companion who is positive and supportive will provide you with constructive feedback that will make you feel there is room for improvement rather than depress you into believing that nothing you ever do is good enough.

Whether it is a relationship at the workplace or a relationship that is far more intimate, we will never find ourselves to be completely similar to other people. Human beings are created equal, but their personality traits and characteristics create altogether different identity groups. It is these differences that allow us to look at the world in a different light, as no two people ever observe things to be a 100% same. The challenge this creates is an inclination towards seeking out people that will conform to our ideals and at least behave or think in the same way as us. Often, such similarities are necessary to form some kind of rapport with others as it puts us in a comfort zone when people see where we are coming from.

Nevertheless, the beauty of life is the way that it contains a plethora of diverse opinions, beliefs, habits, hobbies, and senses of style. Therefore, rather than shying away from those differences, it works in our favor to seek out divergent opinions in order to find ourselves being enriched with a different brand of positivity. It also helps to listen more to others, since by being more receptive to other people's opinions, can we also be heard. Listening actively and with keen interest creates a need within the speaker to talk with more enthusiasm, and it also helps them to boost their self-esteem. Now imagine how it would feel if you would receive the same attention from someone else. It always helps to give as much as you can in order to get the same in return, and only through listening intently can we determine what others think, feel, want, or what they wish to communicate to us.

As we seek to come out of the chasm that we had been left in by our gaslighters, we'll have to utilize a commodity that is quite valuable: time. Because of having spent so much time away from our previous relationships, we will need to catch up and make up for lost time. And it shouldn't be just limited to the cold and mundane ease that technology provides us to reach out to our friends and family. It should also include ensuring your physical, as well as mental and emotional, presence so that others can appreciate that you genuinely wish to make contact. Even though you may have hastily terminated communication with your social circle after the constant pressure from your gaslighter, they should never hold your lapse in judgement against you. And with a concerted and genuine effort to make amends, it is more than likely that they will welcome you back in the fold as they realize you are definitely reaching out to ask for help. Nothing can break the ties that bind, and the distance which you would have traveled with your close friends and family can ensure that they will not let something like a toxic relationship come between you. If anything, they will be more than happy to help you return to normalcy.

Nevertheless, be prepared to get some tough love as well. While you may have had a realization that has finally brought you out of your haze, the ones who care most about you will naturally be inclined to put their two cents in. It doesn't necessarily have to be harsh. Feedback, if coming straight from the heart and with a genuine consideration for your well-being, should be welcome and received with open arms. So long as the language is kept constructive and optimistic rather than full of anger and resentment, feedback from your close friends and family can allow you to tap into your true potential and allow you to get back on track for developing more positive and mutually beneficial relationships.

Gaining feedback also helps you establish a far more important requirement within a relationship: trust. No matter how positive and endearing a relationship can be, it needs to be founded on the basis of mutual trust. Relationships are only as strong as the commitment by both parties to ensure that each other's sanctity is never violated, and trust is by far the easiest to break and difficult to preserve or put back together. Like the precious family vase that your parents tell you never to touch, once it falls and breaks, it will never be the same. Come to think of it, your parent's warnings of staying away from the same vase is essentially a test of trust, one which you can pass only if you are committed to respecting the sanctity of the other person. Vice versa, your trust in the other person should also be reciprocated to keep your secrets safe as well as protecting your being from exploitation either from them or from others.

Lets not forget that the path we are taking to form new and healthy relationships is an exercise in personal development and growth. Each new relationship, ranging from professional to personal, from casual to intimate, can provide us the opportunity to learn something new about the world and the underlying principles of compassion, respect, love, unity, and trust. By seeking out positive and supportive relationships in the family, at home, or in the workplace, we can add a fresh flavor to our lives and learn to be better people. This is all thanks to a sense of happiness and fulfillment we achieve as we feel safe, loved, and appreciated.

Conclusion

By the time you arrive here, you may still be doubting that you are being gaslit. You may strongly believe that the gaslighter is wholly invested in improving the relationship, and therefore they would be able to listen to reason once brought into a calmer setting. And while it isn't bad on your part to consider the possibility that a gaslighter will actually change, it is vital you do not put all your eggs in one basket and instead come up with a backup plan in case things go awry.

Usually, the only way a gaslighter will change is for the worse. Therefore, you must do all you can to build up your resilience against their brand of abuse. Remember that their behavior is not your fault, no matter how much they put the blame on your shoulders. Nothing matters more than your dignity and self-respect, and if a gaslighter is unable to respect your boundaries, then it makes no sense to continue to let them to propagate their toxic agenda over you.

Be warned: A gaslighter doesn't become a master manipulator overnight. They can recognize attempts at having their authority challenged and will no doubt be prepared to counter with moves of their own, as if it were a macabre chess game. They may insinuate that your attempts at establishing boundaries makes you appear insane and unhinged, and they could score bonus points if they point this out in public or in front of your loved ones. However, the key is to not fall for such manipulation and continue to reiterate your self-belief and how you want to change the relationship going forward. It must certainly not be a unilateral decision-making process that is controlled by the gaslighter. Rather, it needs to be a partnership that is based on mutual respect and trust.

Regardless of the relationship dynamic between you and the gaslighter—be it romantic, friendly, professional, or even casually sexual—you need to establish boundaries to protect yourself from mentally and emotionally abusive and debilitating behaviour. If worst comes to worst, you may choose to exercise your personal freedom and distance yourselves from the gaslighter for your own good. Don't forget that the manipulation involved in gaslighting can sow the seeds of doubt within you that will make you wonder if your own self-worth is nothing compared to that of the abusive person in the relationship. Therefore, despite the nature or the rewards that come out of the relationship itself, it is not worth spending even a second more with a person who will only use the relationship to exploit you as much as possible.

Finally, never forget that a gaslighter has taken what you once held most dear, and twisted it for their own benefit. Therefore, it is not at all your fault that you find yourself in such depressing circumstances. However, it is up to you whether or not you wish to stay in such an exploitation cycle full of emotional turmoil and abuse, or to reclaim your identity and your being from the clutches of your abuser to become a happier and healthier you.

If you enjoyed this book in anyway, an honest review is always appreciated!

References

Dean, M. E. (2021, March 16). *What Is Gaslighting? A Sneaky Kind Of Emotional Abuse That Can Harm Your Mental Health*. BetterHelp. https://www.betterhelp.com/advice/relations/gaslighting-a-sneaky-kind-of-emotional-abuse/

Freifeld, L. (2013, March 21). *8 Tips for Developing Positive Relationships*. Training Magazine. https://trainingmag.com/8-tips-for-developing-positive-relationships/

How To Practice Self-Compassion & Be Kind To Yourself (2020, July 7). DiveThru. https://divethru.com/how-to-practice-self-compassion-be-kind-to-yourself/

MSW, J. L., & LCSW. (2019, May 30). On Boundaries: 13 Ways Gaslighting Crosses Boundaries *Out Of My Mind*. https://www.oomm.live/13-ways-gaslighting-crosses-boundaries/

Neff, K. (2019). *Definition and Three Elements of Self Compassion*. https://self-compassion.org/the-three-elements-of-self-compassion-2/

Winch, G. (2016, August 23). *5 ways to build lasting self-esteem*. Ted.com. https://ideas.ted.com/5-ways-to-build-lasting-self-esteem/

www.ingramcontent.com/pod-product-compliance
Lightning Source LLC
Chambersburg PA
CBHW030917080526
44589CB00010B/351